Common Core
La

By

Published by Gallopade International, Inc.
©Carole Marsh/Gallopade
Printed in the U.S.A. (Peachtree City, Georgia)

TABLE OF CONTENTS

G: Includes Graphic Organizer

GO: Graphic Organizer is also available 8½" x 11" online
download at www.gallopade.com/client/go
(numbers above correspond to the graphic organizer numbers online)

What Are Landforms?

Read the text and answer the questions.

> The Earth's surface is what we call land. However, Earth's surface is not flat—it has many unique features of different sizes, shapes, locations, and elevations. The features that make up the Earth's surface, such as mountains, plains, and valleys, are called <u>landforms</u>. Look around outside, and you are sure to see one landform or another.
>
> The Earth has large landforms like mountain ranges, plains, and valleys. However, there are also smaller landforms like pleasant beaches, dark caves, or fan-shaped river deltas. Some landforms, like volcanoes and fault lines, can be violent and destructive. Some of Earth's landforms are underwater on the ocean floor, and some landforms, like an "atoll" or an "isthmus," you may never have heard of before! Did you know that even the continents we live on are a type of enormous landform?
>
> Geologists are scientists who study the Earth, including its landforms. Geologists study a landform's size, shape, and age, but most importantly, geologists study how Earth processes inside and outside the Earth shape the landforms. Some processes, or changes, happen quickly, like the eruption of a volcano, but most changes happen over thousands of years—so slowly that you often cannot see the change occur.

1. A. Use the text to define <u>landform</u>.
   B. What characteristics distinguish one landform from another?

2. Which paragraph—1, 2, or 3—of the text supports each of the following inferences? Cite evidence to support each inference.
   A. _____ Some landforms are large enough to include other landforms.
   B. _____ Many landforms on Earth today were formed long ago.
   C. _____ Landforms come in all shapes and sizes.

3. List at least three adjectives to describe landforms used in paragraph 2.

4. Explain why it is important to study how the Earth changes to understand landforms.

Continents & Oceans

Read the text and answer the questions.

Continents are the largest continuous areas of land above sea level. There are seven continents on Earth: Africa, Antarctica, Asia, Australia, Europe, North America, and South America. Continents contain many familiar smaller landforms such as mountains, valleys, canyons, plains, and many others. Despite how large they are, continents only cover roughly 30% of the Earth's surface.

The Earth's continents are surrounded and separated by the Earth's oceans. The oceans are not truly "landforms," but they can be considered landforms because they are shaped by the land that surrounds them. The five oceans of the world are the Pacific, Atlantic, Indian, Arctic, and Antarctic Oceans. Together, these oceans form one "World Ocean" that covers about 70% of the Earth's surface.

The ocean might also be considered a landform because ocean water rests on top of land. The land underneath the ocean is called the ocean floor. Between continents, the ocean floor swoops downward in a bowl-shaped landform known as an ocean basin. Like continents above water, ocean basins contain many smaller landforms, called ocean floor formations, such as ocean plains, mountain ridges, trenches, and many others.

1. List the seven continents and the five oceans on the Earth's surface.

2. Use information from the text to complete the description wheel for continents and oceans.

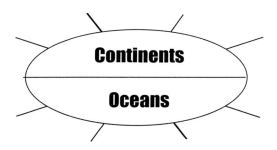

3. Describe the relationship between continents and oceans.

Bumps and Dips

Read the text and answer the questions.

> The Earth's surface is far from flat. The rise and fall of the Earth's surface creates many of the most familiar landforms, including mountains, valleys, plains, and plateaus.
>
> As land rises or falls, it increases or decreases in <u>elevation</u>. Elevation is like height, but elevation is a landform's height above sea level.
>
> Plains are usually flat lands that have a very low elevation. Coastal plains are found near the coasts and often support a wide variety of plant and animal life.
>
> Plateaus are similar to plains. However, plateaus are typically raised above the surrounding land and have a higher elevation. Most plateaus have moderate elevation, but some plateaus are so high, they are too cold for most living things to survive.
>
> Mountains typically have the highest elevations. Mt. McKinley in Alaska has an elevation of 20,320 ft. above sea level—the highest point in the United States! In contrast, a valley is a dip in elevation between two mountains. The lowest point in the United States is found in Death Valley—282 ft. *below* sea level!

1. A. Use the text to define <u>elevation</u>.
    B. Explain how "bumps and dips" are changes in elevation.

2. Explain how a landform, such as Death Valley can be below sea level.

3. With what you just read about elevation, identify each of the landforms on the image below:

    A. _____   B. _____
    C. _____   D. _____

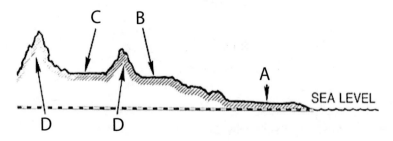

Landforms

Follow the instructions in parts A, B, C, and D.

PART A: Choose one landform to research. Then use online and classroom resources to gather information and images of your landform. Complete the graphic organizer for your landform.

archipelago	canyon	plain	gulf	isthmus
trench	butte	plateau	bay	peninsula
valley	desert	delta	river	lake
volcano	basin	cave	inlet	strait

Landform	Characteristics
Definition	**Examples**

PART B: Organize the information into a digital presentation about your landform. Include details about its shape, size, and distinguishing characteristics. Explain how the landform was formed and where it might be found in the United States.

PART C: Proofread and edit your work. Practice using formal language in your presentation.

PART D: Share your presentation with the class. As a class, categorize these landforms as either land features or water features.

Describing Landforms

Read the text and answer the questions.

Landforms often share many characteristics, but different landforms can be identified and described by their features.

One way to describe landforms is by height. For example, a hill and a mountain both rise high above the surrounding land, but the main difference between a hill and a mountain is height. Mountains are much taller than hills.

Elevation, or distance above sea level, is another important way to describe landforms. The highest elevation in the U.S. is Mount McKinley (20,320 ft. above sea level).

Shape is another way to describe landforms. Some mountains are very rocky, rugged, and rise sharply above the ground. On the other hand, some mountains have gentle slopes, less rocky areas, and have been worn down over time.

Some landforms are described as a group. For example, groups of the same landform have their own name. A group or chain of mountains is called a mountain range. Another example—a group of islands formed close together is called an archipelago.

Some landforms are described by the water that surrounds them. For example, a peninsula is a piece of land that is surrounded by water on three sides. An isthmus is a very narrow strip of land surrounded by water on two sides. An island is an area of land surrounded by water on all sides.

1. A. What is the main idea of this text?
    B. How does the author support the main idea throughout the text?

2. List at least three ways to describe a landform and give at least two examples of each.

3. Complete each analogy with the correct landform.
    state : country   ::   island : _____
    wolf : wolf pack   ::   mountain : _____

4. Which of your five senses is most important for identifying landforms? Explain why.

Describe It!

Look at each image, describe the landform shown, and identify similarities contained by both landforms.

Pictures Courtesy of Wikimedia Commons

Describe It!	Similarities	Describe it!

Courtesy of Wolfgang Moroder (photographer)　　　Courtesy of Wikimedia Commons

Describe It!	Similarities	Describe it!

Landform Regions of North America

Read the text and answer the questions.

1. **Appalachian Mountains**—west of the Coastal Plain, from eastern Canada to Alabama; low-lying eroded mountains; North America's oldest mountain range

2. **Basin and Range**—west of the Rocky Mountains and east of the Sierra Nevada and Cascade mountain ranges; includes varying elevations, and isolated mountain ranges, and Death Valley—the lowest point in North America

3. **Canadian Shield**—horseshoe-shaped area wrapping around Hudson Bay; hills worn by erosion and hundreds of glacier-carved lakes; some of the oldest rock formations in North America

4. **Coastal Plain**—along the Atlantic Ocean and the Gulf of Mexico; broad flat land with many excellent harbors on the coast

5. **Coastal Range**—Pacific Coast stretching from Mexico to Canada; rugged mountains and fertile valleys; several excellent harbors

6. **Great Plains**—west of Interior Lowlands and east of the Rocky Mountains; flat lands that slightly increase in elevation westward; known as grasslands

7. **Interior Lowlands**—west of the Appalachian Mountains and east of the Great Plains; lowlands with rolling flatlands, broad river valleys, and grassy hills

8. **Rocky Mountains**—West of the Great Plains and east of the Basin and Range region; rugged, young mountains with high elevation stretching from Alaska to Mexico; includes Continental Divide

PART A: Use information from the text to answer the questions.

1. Compare and contrast the Coastal Plains and Great Plains.

2. Compare and contrast the Rocky Mountains and Appalachian Mountains in terms of age, location, and physical features.

3. How are the landform regions of the east coast different from the landform regions of the west coast?

4. What makes plains different from lowlands?

5. What can you infer about the climate in the Canadian Shield region? Cite evidence from the text to support your answer.

6. Which regions are most likely suitable for agriculture? Cite evidence from the text to support your answer.

7. When American settlers moved westward, which regions do you think proved the most difficult to cross? Explain your answer with logical reasoning.

PART B: Use the text to identify each region on the map as it is described in the text. Place the number of the region in the correct location on the map.

Geographic Regions of North America

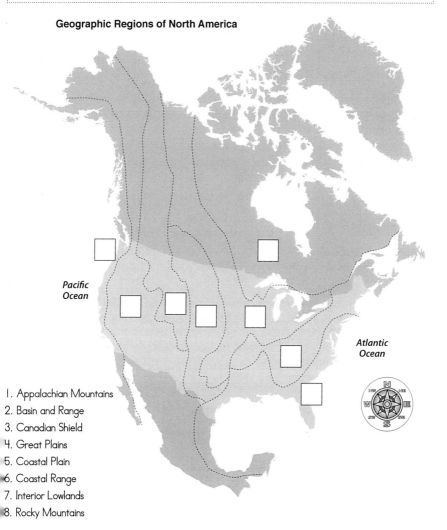

Pacific Ocean

Atlantic Ocean

1. Appalachian Mountains
2. Basin and Range
3. Canadian Shield
4. Great Plains
5. Coastal Plain
6. Coastal Range
7. Interior Lowlands
8. Rocky Mountains

Earth's Moving Crust

Read the text and answer the questions.

The Earth's surface is the very top layer of the Earth's solid crust. Some areas of the crust form the continents, and some areas of the crust form the ocean floors. Underneath the crust is a molten layer of hot magma. The Earth's crust floats on this dense liquid magma, which supports the lighter crust.

Not only does the Earth's crust float, it is broken into sections called tectonic plates. The continents and some ocean basins rest on these tectonic plates. The boundaries of most tectonic plates meet below the ocean. As a plate slowly moves, the continent on it slowly moves too, causing what is known as continental drift.

As the plates move, tectonic plate boundaries pull away from, slide under, shift beside, and collide into each other. The sliding motion of two plate boundaries creates a fault line, or break in the Earth's crust. Areas around a fault experience frequent earthquakes. When plates collide, the edges of the plates are pressed upward forming mountains. Mountains and volcanoes can also be created when one plate slides underneath another plate.

When plates pull away from each other, it opens up cracks in the Earth's crust. Hot magma from below the Earth's crust rises and cools, forming new land on the ocean floor. This process is called sea-floor spreading. Two plates pulling apart can cause earthquakes and form deep ocean trenches. Magma that escapes through the ocean floor can create marine mountain ridges, and even islands.

PART A: Match each vocabulary word from the text to the clue that describes it.

1. _____ Geologic motion caused by tectonic plates

2. _____ Thick molten rock beneath the Earth's crust

3. _____ The most active area of geologic change

4. _____ Part of Earth that includes landforms

5. _____ Parts of the crust that pull, shift, slide, and collide with each other

6. _____ Feature caused by plates sliding past

7. _____ Geologic process cause by two plates pulling apart underneath the ocean

PART B: Use the text to describe the effect of each movement of the Earth's tectonic plates.

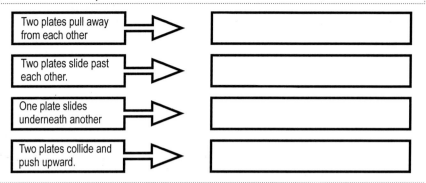

Two plates pull away from each other	⟹	
Two plates slide past each other.	⟹	
One plate slides underneath another	⟹	
Two plates collide and push upward.	⟹	

PART C: Look at the map and answer the questions.

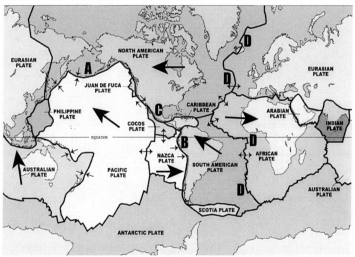

8. A. What does this map show about the Earth's crust?
   B. What do the large arrows on each plate show?
   C. What do the smaller arrows near plate boundaries show?

9. Use what you know about plate tectonics to explain how the group of islands marked A most likely formed.

10. What landforms might be found on the west coast of South America marked B?

11. A fault line marked C runs along the west coast of North America. Describe the movement of the two plates that cause this fault line.

12. The mid-Atlantic ridge (arrows D) is most likely an example of:
    a) a continent   b) sea-floor spreading   c) plate collision

The Landform Report

In small groups, select one of the following categories of landforms: Mountainous, Desert & Plain, Coastal/Oceanic, Volcanic, Artificial/Manmade.

Identify and research 5 different kinds of landforms that fall into your chosen category. Write the name of one of the landforms above each circle. Draw a picture of each of the landforms inside the circles, and describe the landforms on the lines.

Presentation:

1. Organize the information you gathered into a digital presentation.

2. Include images of each landform. Describe what qualities define each landform and explain how each one is formed. What characteristics do the landforms have in common?

3. Give your presentation to the class.

Landforms
Created & Destroyed

Read the text and answer the questions.

It is difficult to guess the age of a landform. That is because many landforms were formed millions of years ago. But that does not mean landforms do not change over time. In fact, landforms are constantly being created and destroyed by Earth processes. Earth processes that slowly tear down landforms are called <u>destructive</u> processes. Earth processes that help to build up landforms are called <u>constructive</u> processes.

Destructive and Constructive Processes

• <u>Weathering</u> is the breaking down or dissolving of Earth's surface rocks and minerals. Weathering does not involve movement.

• <u>Erosion</u> is the process in which earth is worn away, usually by wind, water, or ice. Erosion generally moves rocks and minerals from one place to another.

• <u>Deposition</u> is the process by which soil or rock carried from one place comes to rest in another place. Deposition by wind and rivers help to form beaches, deltas, sand dunes, and fertile soil.

• <u>Tectonic movement</u> is a process that takes place under the Earth's surface. Parts of the Earth's crust shift, slide, and collide, creating new landforms. Tectonic movement causes mountains to push upward over millions of years. It causes volcanoes to erupt, and earthquakes to reveal new land. Faults are where the Earth's crust splits apart, revealing minerals and sediments.

It may seem confusing, but Earth processes can be both constructive and destructive. For example, a volcanic eruption might violently blow the top off a volcanic mountain. However, the lava that runs down the side of a volcano cools and builds the mountain higher. Lava flowing from the ocean floor can form great mountain ridges underwater. If a volcano produces enough lava, this volcanic activity could even reach the ocean's surface and form an island.

1. Constructive and destructive are best described as
    a) synonyms   b) homonyms   c) antonyms   d) metaphors

2. Determine whether each statement is **true** (**T**) or **false** (**F**). What
    evidence from the text supports your answer?
    A. _____ Landforms only change every million years or so.
    B. _____ Erosion and weathering are constructive processes.
    C. _____ Deposition is a constructive process.
    D. _____ Tectonic movement results in both slow and sudden changes
    in Earth's landforms.
    E. _____ Constructive and destructive processes are separate
    processes that do not occur together.

PART B: Read each text. Identify which Earth processes are being
described, and identify each process as constructive, destructive, or both.

The force of a flowing river breaks down bits of rocks and minerals into pebbles,
sand, and soil. As the river carries these pieces toward the ocean, its current
slows and drops the bits of rock, mineral, and soil. Over time, the deposited pieces
of earth build into a fan-shaped river delta at the river's mouth.

3. _____

    _____

    _____

A glacier is an enormous mass of ice. As the glacier slides between mountains, it
scrapes the Earth's surface. The glacier's movement carves steep cliffs into the
mountainsides, which creates a glacial valley.

4. _____

    _____

    _____

Mount Everest is the tallest mountain on Earth, but it is still growing! The tectonic
plates beneath Mount Everest are colliding, pushing the mountain further upward
each year.

5. _____

    _____

    _____

Mesas & Buttes

Read the text and complete the graphic organizer.

Mesas and buttes are flat-topped hills with steep sides. Mesas are usually wider than they are tall. A butte, however, is usually taller than it is wide. Mesas and buttes are two landforms created by the same Earth processes.

Mesas form in an area where tectonic activity has lifted up a large, flat area of land, especially on a plateau. Over time, weathering and erosion from rainfall carve out areas of the uplifted land. However, some rocks are harder and resist the effects of weathering and erosion. A thick layer of hard rock is called a capstone. The hard capstone on top protects the lower layers of rock from the effects of weathering. Over time, the softer rock layers on each side of the capstone are washed away, but not the column of rock beneath the capstone. This creates a wide area of land with a flat top and steep sides—a mesa is born!

A butte is actually just a smaller mesa. Over a long period of time, the mesa's capstone eventually is broken apart by weathering. As the capstone breaks, more and more of the mesa is washed away. The sides of the mesa crumble away until only a small portion of the mesa remains. If the remaining section is taller than it is wide, the landform is called a butte.

1.   What is the difference between a mesa and a butte?

2.   Use the text to number the events in the correct chronological order.
   A.   _____   A butte is formed!
   B.   _____   Areas of hard capstone resist erosion. Soft layers of rock beneath the capstone are protected from weathering and are not broken down by erosion.
   C.   _____   Tectonic activity lifts up a large area of land.
   D.   _____   A mesa is formed!
   F.   _____   Areas of hard capstone eventually erode away.
   G.   _____   More and more pieces of the mesa erode away until the mesa is taller than it is wide!

3.   Which two processes are continually at work during the creation of mesas and buttes? Explain.

Save the Beach!

Read the text and answer the questions.

Sandy Point Community Editorial

1)   Sandy Point has been a pleasant spot for people who want to spend their summer vacation near the beach. Sadly, this little luxury is in danger of vanishing before our eyes!

2)   In the past few years, the winter storms have gotten worse. Powerful winds and waves have carried away much of our beloved beach. The once gently sloping sandy beach is all but gone. The bedrock beneath is beginning to show, and in some places, the remaining sand forms small cliffs that are dangerous to beachgoers.

3)   We, as a community, need to find a solution to this problem or people will stop spending their summers here. Santa Barbara chose to build sea walls to solve a similar problem. However, their problems only got worse—they're losing more beach now than they were before!   One solution presented by the state of Florida is to crush recycled glass into small bits of sand. This "fake" sand could replace what is lost each year, but it just would not feel the same.

4)   As a member of City Council, I am calling all members of our community to contribute their thoughts and ideas to develop a solution to prevent our beach from disappearing forever!

5) Sincerely,
    Jenny Beasley, City Council Coordinator

---

1. A. What problem is presented in this letter?
    B. Which paragraph presents the problem?

2. A. What possible solutions does the author provide?
    B. Describe the author's attitude toward the possible solutions. How do you know?

3. A. What is the stated purpose of this letter?
    B. Why does the author want to achieve that purpose?
    C. Is the author under any pressure to solve the problem at hand?

4. Describe the organization of this letter by explaining the purpose of each section of the letter, 1-5.

Volcanoes

Read the text and answer the questions.

Volcanoes are like mountains, except volcanoes are formed by magma from within the Earth's mantle. The study of how volcanoes form and erupt is called volcanology. The scientists who study volcanoes are called volcanologists.

Most volcanoes form near the edges of tectonic plates. That is because tectonic movement causes cracks in the Earth's crust. Magma from the mantle rises to fill these cracks. Magma can form in small pockets under the Earth's surface, building pressure from underneath. When enough pressure builds, or the magma finds a way to the surface, the volcano erupts!

Magma that reaches the Earth's surface is called lava. The lava cools on the Earth's surface, forming volcanic rocks. Each time a volcano erupts, a new layer of volcanic rock builds the volcano higher and wider. On the ocean floor, volcanoes erupt and cool quickly in the water. Over time, these volcanoes can form massive underwater mountain ranges. Some underwater volcanoes grow large enough to reach the ocean's surface and become volcanic islands. The Hawaiian Islands are a chain of islands formed by volcanic activity.

Volcanoes can be quite dangerous to people who live in cities near a volcano. Hot lava can burn down cities and homes and destroy forests. Even cities far away from a volcano can become covered with soot and ash from an eruption.

1. Use the text to summarize the 5 W's of volcanoes.
   A. What causes volcanoes to form?
   B. Where do volcanoes form?
   C. Who studies volcanoes?
   D. Why is it important to know the effects of volcanic activity?
   E. When does magma become lava?

2. Is volcanic activity a constructive or destructive process? Explain why.

3. A. List at least three effects of volcanic activity on land.
   B. List at least three effects of volcanic activity under water.

In the Cascades

Use the infographic to answer the questions.

The Cascades are a mountain range on the west coast of the United States.

Cascade Eruptions During The Past 4,000 Years

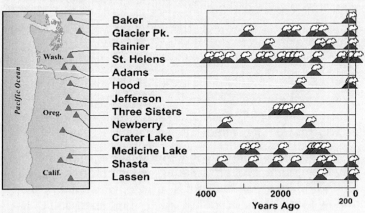

Myers, USGS/CVO, 2000; Modified from: CVO, 1994, USGS Open–File Report 94–585

1. A. Locate the title of this infographic. What information can you gather from the title?
   B. What is the purpose of the map to the left?
   C. What is the purpose of the chart to the right?

2. A. What organization created this infographic?
   B. Why might they have created it?

3. A. Which volcanoes have erupted in the last 200 years?
   B. Which volcano has erupted the most?
   C. Which volcanoes have erupted the least?

4. Read the definitions and answer the questions.

Dormant—describes volcanoes that have not been active in a long time, but could possibly become active again
Extinct—describes volcanoes that are unlikely to erupt again

   A. Which volcanoes are most likely extinct?
   B. Which volcanoes might be dormant?

Fault Lines & Earthquakes

Read the text and answer the questions.

The point where two tectonic plates meet is a landform called a <u>fault line</u>. Fault lines look like cracks in the Earth's surface. Tectonic plates build up immense pressure and energy along the fault lines. The energy is released as the tectonic plates suddenly slip, break apart, or jut upward. The energy released is so strong, it can cause the ground to shift upward, sink downward, or split in two. These sudden movements cause the earth to shake violently— we call that an earthquake.

Some earthquakes can be felt as smaller tremors before the main shock hits. All earthquakes are accompanied by a series of smaller, weaker tremors called "aftershocks."

Despite how fault lines and earthquakes affect humans, they play an important role in creating new landforms. Fault lines cause folds and breaks in the Earth's surface, which are pushed up into new mountains. When two plates pull apart, fault lines can separate, creating basins and canyons. Fault lines along the ocean floor often release magma from the Earth's mantle, forming underwater mountain ranges and even deep ocean trenches.

PART A: Use the text to answer the questions.

1. A. Use the text to define <u>fault line</u>.
   B. Explain why fault lines are examples of constructive Earth processes.

2. A. Earthquakes are a result of what Earth processes?
   B. List at least three possible effects of tectonic movement along a fault line.

3. Why might it be important to know where a fault line is before constructing a house?

4. With a partner, use an online resource to research the San Andreas Fault. What state is it located in? Which two plates form the San Andreas Fault? How has it affected the people living nearby?

PART B: Read the text and answer the questions.

Diary of Jerome B. Clarke, San Francisco, 1906

In every direction from the ferry building, flames were seething, and as I stood there, a five-story building half a block away fell with a crash, and the flames swept clear across Market Street and caught a new fireproof building recently erected. The streets in places had sunk three or four feet, in others great bumps had appeared four or five feet high. The street car tracks were bent and twisted out of shape. Electric wires lay in every direction. Streets on all sides were filled with brick and mortar, buildings either completely collapsed or brick fronts had just dropped completely off. Wagons with horses hitched to them, drivers and all, laying on the streets... these mostly the wagons of produce dealers, who do the greater part of their work at that hour of the morning. Warehouses and large wholesale buildings moved... two or three feet out of the line and still standing with walls all cracked...

Fires were blazing in all directions, and all the finest and best of the office and business buildings were either burning or surrounded. They pumped water from the bay, but fire was soon too far away from the water to make efforts in this direction of much avail. The water mains had been broken by the earthquake, and so there was no supply for the fire engines and they were helpless. The only way out was to dynamite, and I saw some of the finest and most beautiful buildings in the city, new modern palaces, blown to atoms.

5. A. What is being described in this text?
   B. What is the author's purpose for recording this event?
   C. What can you infer about the time of day this event occurred?

6. What geological event occurred before the events described in the text? How do you know?

7. Describe how this event affected each of the following in San Francisco. Cite evidence from the text to support your answers.
   A. the earth's surface   B. human lives   C. buildings

8. Besides the initial event, what other destructive forces affected San Francisco during this event?

9. List at least 5 descriptions that help you "see" and "feel" the event.

10. Compare and contrast the two texts in terms of style, purpose, and detail of information.

11. Citing evidence from both texts, explain how the processes that create Earthquakes are both constructive and destructive.

Human Activity & Landforms

Read the text and answer the questions.

Humans affect landforms almost as much as nature does. Human activities such as mining, drilling, and logging can change the shape of the Earth's surface. Additionally, human activity can affect the Earth processes that shape and change landforms.

Humans cut down trees from mountainsides to use in many different ways. Mountainsides that have been cleared of trees and other plants are more likely to have landslides during a heavy rain. Without trees, winds easily blow away the top layers of soil.

Humans change the natural course of water by damming rivers and building canals. These structures can cause some rivers and lakes to dry up. Damming a river floods a valley or basin and turns it into a lake. Building canals and dams can lessen the effects of water erosion, causing fewer minerals and nutrients to be brought from high elevations to the coastal plains and lowlands.

Humans also mine deep underground, which can weaken the crust's structure and cause sinkholes (collapsed earth). The same can be applied to offshore mining operations and with these, an accident might pollute the surrounding ocean for miles, ruining wildlife and possibly even beaches.

Identify at least 5 ways that humans affect the landforms on the Earth's surface and describe the effect.

Cause:	Effect:
Cause:	Effect:
Cause:	Effect:
Cause:	Effect:
Cause:	Effect: